Canadian Citizenship

D1064219

Weigl Educational Publishers Limited

Published by Weigl Educational Publishers Limited
6325 – 10 Street SE
Calgary, Alberta, Canada
T2H 2Z9

Web site: www.weigl.com
Copyright 2005 WEIGL EDUCATIONAL PUBLISHERS LIMITED

All of the Internet URLs given in the book were valid at the time of publication.
However, due to the dynamic nature of the Internet, some addresses may have
changed, or sites may have ceased to exist since publication. While the author and
publisher regret any inconvenience this may cause readers, no responsibility for any
such changes can be accepted by either the author or the publisher.

Library and Archives Canada Cataloguing in Publication
    Canadian citizenship / Don Wells, editor.
(Canadian government)
Includes index.
ISBN 1-55388-097-8 (bound) ISBN 1-55388-122-2 (pbk)
    1. Citizenship--Canada--Textbooks. 2. Civil rights--Canada--Textbooks. I.
Wells, Don, 1953- II. Series: Canadian government (Calgary, Alta.)
JL187.C274 2004   323'.0971   C2004-903626-2

Printed in the United States of America
1 2 3 4 5 6 7 8 9 0   09 08 07 06 05 04

We acknowledge the
financial support of the
Government of Canada
through the Book
Publishing Industry
Development Program
(BPIDP) for our
publishing activities.

Editor
Don Wells

Copy Editor
Tina Schwartzenberger

Photo Researcher
Ellen Byran

Designer
Warren Clark

Layout
Terry Paulhus

On the Cover
Canadian athletes
enter the Olympic
Stadium at the 2004
Summer Olympics in
Athens, Greece

Contents

Canadian Citizenship 4

Rights and Freedoms 6

Citizens' Responsibilities 8

The Charter of Rights and Freedoms 10

Making the Charter Work 12

Provincial Human Rights Protection 14

Human Rights Commissions 16

Violated Rights 18

Minority Rights During War 20

Women and Discrimination 22

Aboriginal Peoples and Discrimination 24

Mapping Canada's Immigrants 26

Fostering Tolerance 28

Becoming a Canadian Citizen 30

Participatory Citizenship 32

Lobbying 34

Government Response to Participation 36

Media and Politics 38

Universal Declaration of Human Rights 40

Time Line 42

Quiz 44

Further Research 46

Glossary 47

Index 48

Canadian Citizenship

The people of a country are called its citizens. They share that country's laws, traditions, and beliefs with their fellow citizens. Citizens also have specific **rights** and **responsibilities**.

A Canadian citizen is either born in Canada or has sworn or affirmed the oath of Canadian **citizenship** in front of a citizenship judge. Generally, once you are or become a Canadian citizen, you remain a Canadian citizen for the rest of your life.

All Canadian citizens have equal rights and privileges. As a Canadian citizen, you have the right to vote and to be a candidate in federal and provincial elections. You have the freedom to enter, remain in, or leave Canada. You have the right to work and live in any province or territory you choose as well as the right to carry a Canadian passport.

Canadian citizens have several important responsibilities. They must be loyal to their country, to the Queen and Her representatives, and to the governor general and lieutenant governors. Canadian citizens must obey Canada's laws, respect the rights and property of others, care for the country's **heritage**, and support its ideals.

Canadian citizenship includes both rights and responsibilities. The Charter of Rights and Freedoms is the supreme law of our country. It guarantees the

The citizenship ceremony marks a new Canadian's official entrance to Canada.

rights of all people living in Canada and describes the specific rights of Canadian citizens. Other legislation and agencies also protect Canadian citizens' rights. The passing of the Charter of Rights and Freedoms in 1982 changed Canada from a parliamentary **democracy**, in which governments could limit rights and freedoms at its discretion, into a constitutional democracy, which more effectively restrains governments from denying rights and freedoms. Understanding the Charter and what it means to Canadians is essential to the idea of citizenship.

A look at the history of **prejudice** and **discrimination** in Canada reveals how the rights and responsibilities of Canadians have changed dramatically throughout the twentieth century. Governments and citizens are continually working toward the goal of a tolerant society in which all people live freely and participate equally without discrimination.

Participation is a key responsibility of Canadian citizens. Canadians have many opportunities to contribute to the quality of life in our country as individuals or members of their communities. In your daily life, you acquire knowledge, skills, and attitudes by reading the newspaper, listening to or watching the news, and talking with your friends and family about issues that concern you. In turn, you act on your knowledge, skills, and attitudes by exercising your rights and responsibilities as a Canadian citizen. You can vote, write a letter to a politician or government official, become active in your community, join a **political party**, or run for political office.

Non-Canadian citizens living in Canada have the same legal rights and the same responsibility to obey the law as Canadian citizens do. However, only citizens enjoy the political right to participate fully in the democratic life of this country.

July 1 is a day when Canadians celebrate their country and its people.

Rights and Freedoms

A right is something to which people are entitled simply because they are human beings.

People often talk about the right to equality, the right to life, and the right to free expression. Rights are not gifts or privileges, and they cannot be earned or purchased.

Some rights belong to every individual, such as the right to life, liberty, and personal security. These are called natural human rights. In Canada and elsewhere around the world, natural human rights are considered essential to human dignity. **Human rights** are an abstract ideal, not a guarantee. Each society must secure and protect the freedoms it values through the laws it adopts. A society must enforce those laws through its legal and judicial systems.

The idea of all people having rights is a relatively recent one in the history of western civilization. In medieval times, only landowners had rights. Peasants had no rights and lived entirely subject to their lords. In the last century, the United States had slavery, a condition in which African Americans had no rights. In the last 50 years, Canadian women and Aboriginal

HISTORY

Development of Citizens' Rights

In the thirteenth century, a group of nobles forced King John of England to sign the Magna Carta in order to protect themselves from arbitrary acts by the king. The Magna Carta included some fundamental rights, such as trial by jury. These rights protected the nobles against the arbitrary taking of life, liberty, or property, which kings such as John felt was their divine right.

These protections against the **power** of the king were originally intended for the privileged classes. Over time, they became the rights of all English people, and they were used in other documents. The Magna Carta established the principle that the power of the monarchy was not absolute.

The Magna Carta was respected by some monarchs and ignored by others. From 1215 to 1628, England's **Parliament** slowly gained power. By 1628, when Charles I asked Parliament to raise taxes, it refused until he signed the Petition of Rights. The Petition built on the principles contained in the Magna Carta and challenged the idea

■ *The Lincoln Cathedral, Salisbury Cathedral, and the British Museum have the four original copies of the Magna Carta.*

of the divine right of kings. The Petition made it plain that even a monarch must obey the law of the land.

In 1689, the English **Bill** of Rights went further in limiting the power of the monarchy and protecting the rights of individuals. The Bill of Rights said that elections for Parliament should be held on a regular basis. It reaffirmed the right to a trial by jury and protected people from excessive fines and cruel or unjust punishment. It allowed citizens to bear arms, and it established the right of *habeas corpus*, the idea that a person must be charged with a specific crime before being imprisoned.

■ **More than 10 million Canadians are descended from ancestors who belonged to more than one ethnic group.**

Peoples had only limited rights.

Today, most western countries support the idea that all people have natural human rights. In Canada, the Charter of Rights and Freedoms guarantees fundamental freedoms to all people in Canada. These include the freedom of thought, conscience and religion, the freedom of expression, the freedom to assemble peacefully, and the freedom to associate with whom you please. These freedoms protect individuals from unjustified and improper government action and allow individuals to live as they choose.

The Charter also guarantees certain other rights of Canadians. Different from fundamental freedoms, these rights are not intended to protect individuals from government actions; instead, they describe how individuals live

and participate in society. For example, democratic rights entitle a country's citizens to control and direct their government by voting in elections. Every country has a slightly different idea of what rights are and makes laws to protect the rights of its citizens.

In Canada, our rights include the right to move freely in and out of the country, the right to be treated without discrimination before the law, and the right to speak one of Canada's two official languages. One of the most important rights is the right of citizens to vote for a new government at least once every 5 years. It is the government's obligation to call an election within this time period.

▼ **FURTHER UNDERSTANDING**

Natural Human Rights

According to this political theory, all human beings have certain rights that governments cannot take away from them. These rights include the right to worship, the right to have a say in government, and the right of property. This theory is based on the ancient idea of Natural Law, which states that people are creatures of nature and God, and they must live by the rules of nature or God. Natural human rights are expressed in the English Bill of Rights (1689), the American Declaration of Independence (1776), the French Declaration of the Rights of Man and the Citizen (1789), the first ten amendments to the Constitution of the United States (known as the Bill of Rights 1791), and the United Nations' Universal Declaration of Human Rights (1948).

Citizens' Responsibilities

Canadians have many rights, but they also have responsibilities, or duties they are obliged to perform. Some responsibilities are clearly stated in our laws. Others are expressed indirectly, or they are implied. A person who becomes a Canadian citizen takes an oath that includes the legal responsibilities shared by every Canadian citizen. Canadians must be loyal to Canada, obey Canadian laws, respect the rights of others, care for Canada's heritage, and support Canada's ideals. These ideals include policies of multiculturalism and equality.

As long as the government does not interfere with people's rights, it has the authority to make laws. Citizens have a responsibility to respect the government's authority to make laws and the duty to observe those laws. Canadian citizens benefit from economic, medical, and education support. With those rights comes the legal responsibility to pay taxes. Canadians have the right to equality before the law and equal protection under the law. As a result, citizens are legally obligated to do jury duty when required.

Citizens must exercise and defend not only their own rights, but also the rights of others. They have an obligation to contribute to the welfare of society as

ACTIVE CITIZENSHIP

Awarding Responsible Citizens

On July 1, 1967, on the 100th anniversary of Canada's Confederation, the government created an award, called the Order of Canada, to honour Canadians who have enriched the lives of others. There are three levels of membership for the Order of Canada: companion, officer, and member. The companion award is given for international achievement. The officer award is given for national achievement. The member award is given for contributions at the local or regional level. Recipients may use special letters after their names to indicate their status: CC (companion of the order), OC (officer of the order), and

CM (member of the order). Recipients are also given a badge and ribbons to wear on special occasions and a small pin to wear with everyday clothes. The badge and pin are made up of a snowflake, a crown, a maple leaf, and a Latin motto that means "They desire a better country."

Other awards that attract national attention are the annual Governor General's Literary Awards, which recognize and reward

More than 4,000 people have been awarded the Order of Canada since 1967.

Canadian writers. These awards are given to English- and French-language works selected as the best in each of the following six categories: fiction, non-fiction, drama, poetry, children's literature, and translation. Winners receive a medal from the governor general, $15,000, and a specially bound copy of their award-winning work.

Fire protection within a city or town is the responsibility of the municipal government. Forest fires, on the other hand, fall under the responsibility of the provincial or territorial government.

FURTHER UNDERSTANDING

Multiculturalism

Multiculturalism is a term used to describe societies with many different cultures. Biculturalism, or a society with two cultures, was Canada's official policy until the 1960s. Aboriginal groups and the Chinese community, among others, objected to the bicultural view and favoured the term multiculturalism. In 1971, Pierre Trudeau made multiculturalism Canada's official policy. This policy was included in the 1982 Constitution. Multicultural policies around the world include:

- dual citizenship,
- government support for minority language newspapers, television, and radio,
- support for minority festivals, holidays, and celebrations,
- tolerance of traditional or religious dress in schools, the military, and society in general,
- support for art from other cultures, and
- programs to encourage minorities to participate in politics, education, and the work force.

a whole by participating in their communities or in our political system. Voting in federal and provincial elections is a right. Many people consider it their responsibility to vote and thereby participate in and uphold the democratic process.

Government has its own responsibilities to the people. The federal government is responsible for matters that affect all Canadians, such as citizenship, national defence, foreign policy, national economic policy, currency, and postal services. Provincial and territorial governments are responsible for areas that concern all people who live in a province or territory, such as education, highways, health care, child welfare, and workers' compensation. Municipal governments are responsible for matters that affect local areas, such as building regulations, parks and recreation, fire protection, and municipal libraries. Sometimes governments share responsibilities for the same areas, for example, justice, the protection of human rights, the environment, and immigration.

9

The Charter of Rights and Freedoms

The Charter of Rights and Freedoms outlines Canadians' fundamental freedoms and a number of specific rights.

■ *Some teenagers feel that they are discriminated against because of their age.*

FURTHER UNDERSTANDING

Limits on the Freedom of Speech

The Charter of Rights and Freedoms guarantees Canadians the freedom of speech. However, there are limits on what a person may say or write. A person can be sued if he or she says (slander) or writes (libel) something untrue about another person and ruins his or her reputation. A person can be charged with a criminal offence if he or she says or writes something that promotes hatred against an identifiable group. Sexual remarks or teasing can be considered sexual harassment. A person can be charged with public mischief if he or she yells "Fire!" in a crowded theatre as a joke.

The rights of Canadians gained legal protection when the Canadian Charter of Rights and Freedoms was passed in 1982. Unless specifically excluded, every federal and provincial law is limited by the rights and freedoms guaranteed in the Charter. Until 1982, the rights and freedoms of Canadian citizens were not written laws collected in one place. Instead, they were passed down as valued customs and traditions in our society or were scattered throughout many different laws and documents. Now that the Charter is part of Canada's Constitution, it can be changed only by special amendment procedures involving the federal and provincial governments.

The Charter helps balance government power and individual freedom. The Charter is Canada's supreme law. Government cannot violate the rights and freedoms of Canadians.

Today, citizens who feel their rights have been denied can seek protection from a court of law. The courts have the final say regarding the scope and extent of Canadians' rights.

The Charter of Rights and Freedoms outlines Canadians' fundamental freedoms and a number of specific rights. The Charter addresses five groups of rights: democratic rights, mobility rights, legal rights, equality rights, and language rights. Some of these apply only to citizens, while some apply to everyone living in Canada.

The Canadian Charter of Rights and Freedoms

Guarantee of Rights and Freedoms

The rights and freedoms in the Charter are guaranteed. The government is allowed to pass laws to limit our freedoms, but these limits must be reasonable and justifiable in a court of law. This means there must be a balance between citizens' rights and freedoms and the good of society.

Fundamental Freedoms

The basic freedoms of all citizens are guaranteed: freedom of conscience and religion; freedom of thought, belief, opinion, and expression; freedom of peaceful assembly; freedom of association; and freedom of the press and media.

Democratic Rights

Canadian citizens have the right to vote. The House of Commons and the legislative assemblies are limited to 5-year terms, except during times of war. During a war, the government must get a two-thirds majority vote in the House of Commons to extend its term.

Mobility Rights

Canadian citizens are free to enter, leave, and move around in Canada as they wish. All citizens have equal access to services in all provinces and territories.

Legal Rights

The legal rights of citizens, including life, liberty, and the security of person, are guaranteed. Citizens have additional rights with respect to arrest, searches, imprisonment, legal counsel, trials, and some court procedures.

Equality Rights

All citizens are equal with respect to the law. All citizens receive equal protection by the law, regardless of race, ethnic or national origin, colour, religion, gender, age, or mental or physical disability.

Official Languages of Canada

English and French are Canada's official languages. Both languages have equal status, rights, and privileges in all federal institutions and Parliament. French and English are also New Brunswick's official languages, with equal status, rights, and privileges. Canadian citizens can obtain all federal government services and New Brunswick government services in either English or French. Citizens have the right to use either English or French in federal courts.

Enforcement

The courts will enforce the rights and freedoms of citizens.

General

Nothing in the Charter will lessen existing rights of Canada's Aboriginal Peoples. The Charter will be applied to enhance the multicultural nature of Canada. The rights and freedoms in the Charter are guaranteed equally to males and females. There may be additional rights and freedoms not listed in the Charter.

Application of Charter

The Charter states where and to whom it applies. The Charter gives Parliament and the provincial and territorial legislatures some power to limit the legal rights, equality rights, and fundamental freedoms of citizens.

Making the Charter Work

When the Charter became law in 1982, federal and provincial governments reviewed existing laws and changed anything that directly infringed upon the rights and freedoms described in the Charter. However, conflicts between government authority and human and civil rights are not always easy to resolve. The Charter recognizes that government laws and activities frequently infringe upon people's rights. The Charter provides a solution to such conflicts by letting the courts decide when interference with the rights of individuals or groups is not acceptable and when it is appropriate for the good of all people. The courts examine each case of conflict between a government action and a particular right or freedom. The courts can strike down laws that infringe on Charter rights and freedoms. However, it remains the responsibility of governments to create laws that are sensitive to the Charter.

Individual Canadians have also challenged many existing laws that deny the rights of some individuals and groups. Citizens have brought numerous test cases before the Supreme Court to challenge the law or raise new questions that have not been previously addressed. Such challenges are essential in making the Charter work. Many citizens have fought for their rights using their own resources. Legal action groups have been created to help individuals test the laws on a variety of issues.

It was just a matter of time before Justine Blainey became known for her skills on the ice instead of her gender.

ACTIVE CITIZENSHIP

Margaret Atwood

Margaret Atwood has earned a reputation as one of Canada's most skilled writers. She also takes an active interest in civil rights and social issues. Atwood has worked on behalf of Amnesty International and has campaigned in favour of protecting the environment. Her efforts have influenced government decisions and touched people across the country.

Born in Ottawa in 1939, Atwood started telling stories at a young age. Later in life, Atwood became an award-winning poet and novelist. Her first poetry book won a Governor General's Award in 1966, and her novels have been praised by critics around the world.

Atwood developed a strong interest in civil rights and social issues. She spent years as an active member of Amnesty International, an experience that influenced some of her later writing.

Atwood has also campaigned in favour of preserving natural areas. Her strong appreciation of nature emerged during childhood. She grew up in northern Québec where her

"Unless we behave differently as individuals, the bad news will keep getting worse."

father, an entomologist, studied insects that feed on healthy trees.

In the 1980s, Atwood grew concerned when timber companies revealed plans to build two logging roads through the Temagami area north of North Bay, Ontario. The area was described by a Toronto

newspaper as "hauntingly beautiful, much as it was some 60 years ago." Temagami featured a network of canoe routes, and canoe trips produced nearly $1.6 million annually for area businesses. The Temagami area was close to where Atwood grew up, and the author became angry that Ontario's government seemed to support plans for road development.

Although the timber companies argued that the roads would save hundreds of jobs, Atwood said loggers should keep their distance from popular tourist destinations. She said people who fish, hunt, and sightsee would be deterred by logging roads, and the long-term consequences of clearing hectares of trees could be serious.

In 1988, Atwood wrote an article for the *Toronto Star* newspaper on how individuals can make a difference by taking action against pollution. "The Great Lakes are the world's largest toxic sewer," she wrote. "Unless we behave differently as individuals, the bad news will keep getting worse."

For example, in 1985, 12-year-old Justine Blainey was the first girl chosen to play hockey in the Metro Toronto Hockey League. The Ontario Hockey Association barred her from playing in the league, claiming the league was for boys only. The existing human rights law supported the league's right to have separate boys' and girls' teams. With the help of the Women's Legal Education and Action Fund (LEAF), Justine challenged the law, claiming it violated the section of the Charter that prohibits discrimination based on gender. The Ontario Court of Appeal agreed that the law was discriminatory. Justine then challenged the Ontario Hockey Association's policy before the Ontario Human Rights Commission. The Ontario Human Rights Commission eventually declared sex discrimination in athletic activities unlawful in Ontario.

Provincial Human Rights Protection

When Canadian men went to fight in World War II, women took their places in the workplace.

Provinces also pass laws to protect their citizen's rights. In the 1930s, many provinces began enacting laws to prohibit discrimination against people in the workplace and against certain disadvantaged groups in society.

In the 1950s, provinces began passing laws for fair employment and equal pay. Provincial lawmakers drew upon the general principles of human rights to create this type of human rights legislation. Human rights laws underline the belief that all people should have an equal opportunity to create the type of life they are able and

wish to have without being hindered by discrimination. By 1975, all provinces had similar laws in place and had set up human rights commissions to study complaints about discrimination.

As with the provincial, territorial, and federal governments, in addition to the Canadian Charter of Rights and Freedoms, Alberta has two laws that protect human rights: the Alberta Bill of Rights and the Individual's Rights Protection Act (IRPA).

Passed in 1972, the Individual's Rights Protection Act is not intended to control what people think about others

DOCUMENT

The Alberta Individual's Rights Protections Act (excerpt)

As with other provinces and territories, Alberta's Individual's Rights Protection Act protects people from discrimination and unfair practices. The IRPA protects citizens on many grounds, including those related to employment; job advertisements, applications and interviews, tenancy, public services, accommodation, and signs and notices. Under the IRPA, it is against the law to discriminate against people on these grounds: race or ancestry; places of origin; country of birth outside Canada; colour; religion; physical disability, infirmity, or disfigurement; gender; age (18 or older); or marital status.

The Alberta human rights law contains provisions that ensure individuals are not discriminated against when seeking a job or a place to live:

Discrimination Regarding Public Accommodation

3   No person directly or indirectly, alone or with another, [alone] or by interpostion of another, shall
(a)   deny to any person or class of persons any accommodation, services or facilities customarily available to the public, or
(b)   discriminate against any person or class of persons with respect to any accommodation, services or facilities customarily available to the public, because of race, religious beliefs, colour, gender, physical disability, ancestry or place of origin of that person or class of persons or of any other person or class of persons.

Discrimination Regarding Employment Practices

7(1) No employer or person acting on behalf of an employer shall
(a)   refuse to employ or refuse to continue to employ, or
(b)   discriminate against any person with regard to employment or any term or condition of employment because of race, religious beliefs, colour, gender, physical disability, marital status, age, ancestry, or place of origin of that person or any other person.

(prejudice), but to prohibit what people do with their prejudice (discrimination). Unlike the Charter, the Individual's Rights Protection Act can be changed by the Alberta Legislature. The Act does not provide a constitutional guarantee to Albertans. The Act protects individuals from the discriminatory actions of government and ensures that individuals do not discriminate against others.

Specifically, the IRPA protects Albertans from discrimination in employment, employment applications and advertisements, tenancy, public services, and public signs and notices. The Act prohibits discrimination on the basis of race, religious beliefs, colour, gender, physical disability, ancestry, and place of origin. In matters of employment, it forbids discrimination on the basis of age (for people eighteen and over), marital status, and pregnancy. The exceptions to these employment regulations are when individuals work in a private home or work on a farm and live in the farmer's home. Sexual harassment is also considered discrimination.

All of Canada's provinces and territories have laws that ensure equal opportunity, freedom from discrimination, freedom to earn a living, and the right to have a place to live and enjoy public services and accommodation.

Human Rights Commissions

Between the years 1988 and 1997, the Human Rights Commission received 7,450 signed complaints. Only 6 percent of these complaints went to the human rights tribunal.

Most provinces have human rights commissions to make sure all their citizens have the same rights and freedoms. Most human rights commissions have the power to take individuals to court, although they usually try to settle complaints out of court.

Most provincial human rights commissions are bound by the laws of their provinces. In Alberta, individuals who feel they have been discriminated against may complain to the Alberta Human Rights Commission. The Alberta Human Rights Commission was formed in 1973 to enforce the Individual's Rights Protection Act.

The Commission is comprised of seven members appointed by the lieutenant governor. The Commission is an independent body, but it reports to the province's minister of labour.

In responding to a complaint, if the Commission finds that discrimination has occurred, it begins an investigation. Human Rights Commission officers solve problems by first trying to arrange an agreeable solution between the two sides. If this fails, the Commission can ask the province's minister of labour to appoint a board of inquiry to explore the matter further.

The Alberta Human Rights Commission can only take action if

there is an act of discrimination that is covered by IRPA. This means that the Commission can only help individuals who experience discrimination prohibited by Alberta's human rights legislation. For example, it is legal for an employer to refuse to hire a 17-year-old because he or she is too young. In this type of case, the Human Rights Commission cannot do anything to help. If, however, an employer refuses to hire a 70-year-old man because he is too old, the Commission can get involved.

Human rights commissions also educate the public about human rights issues in general and the specifics of provincial legislation. The commissions teach people how to use the law to help themselves and increase public understanding and tolerance through education.

Laws such as the Individual's Rights Protection Act cannot prevent prejudice. If an individual complains to a human rights commission about prejudice, there is little the commission can do beyond education. Through education, human rights commissions hope to change prejudice and, therefore, discrimination.

Freedom of Religion and Conscience

Many Canadians take freedom of religion for granted because their beliefs and lifestyles are similar to the majority. However, other Canadians have experienced difficulty because their beliefs are very different from those of the majority of Canadians.

The first Canadian Hutterite colonies were established on the Prairies in 1918. The Hutterites lived in colonies and farmed the land. Bound together by deep Christian faith, they sought a simple life on the land, rejecting the violence and technology of the outside world.

Years earlier, the Hutterites fled religious persecution in Czechoslovakia, their home

country, and moved to Hungary, Romania, Russia, and the United States. In the United States, they were harassed for refusing to join the military, and they migrated to Canada.

The Hutterites soon became prosperous farmers. However, feelings toward the Hutterites began to change

■ *Most Hutterite colonies produce their own food. As a result, they spend little money in local communities.*

when World War II started. The Hutterites were against war, and they did not volunteer to fight. Instead, they volunteered for forestry and road construction work. Some people began to grumble that the Hutterites were not doing their part for Canada.

In 1944, the Alberta government enacted a law that kept Hutterites from buying or leasing new land. The Land Sales Prohibition Act was meant to last only during the war. The government said the law would protect the Hutterites from violence if they moved into new areas where their anti-war philosophy was unpopular.

Independent farmers blocked an attempt to repeal the law, and it was replaced in 1947 with the Communal Property Act. This Act prohibited Hutterite colonies from buying more than 2,590 hectares of land or locating a new colony within 64 kilometres of an existing colony.

During the 1960s, attitudes began to change. Prejudice became less acceptable in Canada. The country began to develop a multicultural policy, and provinces began to establish human rights laws. In 1972, the Communal Properties Act was repealed.

Violated Rights

Prejudice and discrimination are closely connected.

Today, it is assumed that the government protects people's rights and freedoms in our country. Yet individuals belonging to minority groups do not always have the same opportunities as other Canadians to participate in politics, social activities, and work.

Prejudice and discrimination are closely connected. Prejudice consists of what people think. Literally, it means judging in advance. Usually people talk about prejudice in a negative way and associate it with unfairness, a lack of openness, and intolerance. Prejudice results from forming an opinion without carefully considering the facts. Prejudice can be learned, for example, when children repeat the ideas of their parents. Prejudice can be eradicated through awareness and education.

Discrimination is how people act based on their ideas or prejudices. Discrimination can be positive. For example, a person with good taste is said to be "discriminating." When people talk about discriminating against a person or a group, they use it in a negative way.

Even though Canadian laws protect people against discrimination, it still exists in some of the values and traditions of our society and in the rules and practices of some institutions. This is a subtle type of discrimination that has the same long-term effects on groups and communities who have been openly denied full and equal participation in Canada's recent history.

At different times in Canadian history, groups of people have been denied their rights and have been subject

Approximately 15,000 Chinese labourers worked to complete the British Columbia section of the Canadian Pacific Railroad. More than 600 Chinese labourers died on the job.

HISTORY

Canada's Immigration Policy to stop Asians

In 1908, the Canadian government's immigration policy required immigrants to come to Canada without stopping on the journey from their country of origin. This almost completely stopped immigration from India. The distance from India to Canada made it difficult to travel without stopping along the way. In 1910, the policy was changed to restrict the immigration of the wives and children of people already living in Canada.

In 1914, after a 2-month voyage, 376 Indians, mostly Sikhs, sailed into Vancouver harbour on the steamer *Komagata Maru* to test the

government ruling. British Columbia newspapers said the mostly adult male immigrants were "sick," "hungry," "undesirable," and "a menace to women and children."

When the ship arrived in British Columbia, the Indian

immigrants were not allowed to leave the ship. The ship sat in the harbour for 2 months. During this time, there were attempts to intimidate and force the passengers off the steamer so they could be deported. Finally, the ship returned to India. With the

■ *Today, more than 147,000 Sikhs live in Canada.*

exception of around twenty returning residents and the ship's doctor, no passengers were allowed to leave the ship.

to unequal treatment in Canadian society. A good example is the Chinese immigrants who helped build the Canadian Pacific Railway (CPR).

In the late 1850s, Chinese immigrants began settling in British Columbia. In the 1870s, the Canadian Pacific Railway brought 17,000 Chinese workers to Canada. CPR paid these Chinese workers low wages to build the railroad linking eastern and western Canada. Many Chinese railway workers died from the harsh and unsafe conditions before the railway was completed in 1885.

By 1891, some of the workers had returned to China, but the majority decided to stay in Canada. Some people in British Columbia objected to Chinese

immigration and were uneasy about the different culture and beliefs of the Chinese. The Canadian government decided to slow further immigration from China by taxing new Asian immigrants. In 1923, the government passed a law that effectively prohibited immigration from Asian countries. Only in 1967 did the government remove all restrictions on Chinese immigration.

The Chinese community not only suffered because of low wages and discrimination in immigration, but for many years Chinese people could not practise particular professions, such as law, medicine, or accounting. Chinese people sought an apology from the Canadian government and a cash settlement.

Minority Rights During War

During World War I (1914–1918), the Canadian government acted to protect the public from what it believed were enemy sympathizers living in Canada. Many Ukrainians had come to Canada from the Austrian Empire, so they were classified as "enemy aliens."

The government moved more than 8,000 Ukrainian Canadians from their homes in western Canada to work camps and forced more than 88,000 to report their whereabouts regularly to government authorities.

Despite this discrimination, up to 10,000 Ukrainian Canadians enlisted in the Canadian army to aid the war effort. Many of those who enlisted had to change their names and hide their cultural origins.

During World War II (1939–1945), Japanese Canadians faced even more discrimination than Ukrainians faced in World War I. The Canadian government removed the rights and freedoms of Japanese Canadians by using the War Measures Act. This denial of rights was one of the most serious cases of discrimination ever to occur in Canada. It had long-term effects on the Japanese-Canadian community and remains an issue today.

The Japanese first came to Canada at the end of the nineteenth century, after trading began between Canada and Japan. Most Japanese immigrants settled on the coast of British Columbia, especially in the cities of Vancouver and Victoria. During the late 1890s and early 1900s, Japanese immigration increased.

Resentment of the Japanese grew among some people in British Columbia. Some felt the Japanese, and some other races, should not be allowed to immigrate to Canada. These people

In 1942, 22,000 Japanese Canadians were taken from their homes and relocated to eight internment camps in the interior of British Columbia.

were afraid the Japanese would take jobs away from people already living in Canada. Some people were afraid of the highly developed Japanese culture. Others felt that the Japanese people were inferior to Europeans.

Government policies in British Columbia encouraged anti-Japanese feelings. Japanese Canadians were denied the right to vote and were prevented from practising most professions, including working in the civil service and teaching.

In World War II, Japan allied with Germany. Canada joined Great Britain in the war against Germany. This made Japan an enemy of Canada. Japanese Canadians were viewed, therefore, as enemies of Canada.

Feelings of hostility toward Japanese Canadians grew rapidly, especially after Japan bombed the American naval base at Pearl Harbor, Hawaii, in December 1941. In February 1942, the Canadian government ordered the removal of all Japanese Canadians from the area within 160 kilometres of the Pacific coast. The Canadian government believed Canada's security was threatened by the presence of the Japanese near the coast.

Some Canadians felt Japanese Canadians were being treated unfairly. Senior members of the military and Royal Canadian Mounted Police (RCMP) protested the action, saying the Japanese Canadians posed no threat. No Japanese Canadian was ever charged with disloyalty to Canada.

More than 20,000 Japanese Canadians were moved by the government. At first, they were moved into livestock barns at the Pacific National Exhibition grounds in Vancouver. Then they were moved into

hastily-built camps where they lived until the war ended. Thousands of displaced men, women, and children were forced to live in the interior of British Columbia, in southern Alberta, and elsewhere. Others were sent back to Japan. The government sold their homes, farms, businesses, and personal property.

After the war ended in 1945, some Japanese Canadians stayed where they had been moved by the government. Some returned to British Columbia and the west coast. Even in 1948, however, Japanese Canadians received prison sentences for trying to return to their homes in British Columbia. Public opinion prevented the government from sending more Japanese Canadians to Japan. Japanese Canadians did not receive the right to vote until 1949.

In 1984, Prime Minister Brian Mulroney promised Canadians that he would compensate Japanese Canadians for their losses during World War II. In September 1988, after 4 years of discussion with members of the Japanese-Canadian community, a settlement was finalized.

Living conditions in the interment camps were very rough. Japanese Canadians had to survive with the few things they were able to take with them.

FURTHER UNDERSTANDING
War Measures Act

The War Measures Act was passed in August of 1914. It was designed to transfer many powers from Parliament to the federal cabinet. This allowed Canada to meet the emergency of World War I. The law was similar to the Defence of the Realm Act passed by the Parliament of Great Britain. The British law was repealed in 1918, but the Canadian law remained. This Act was used in 1939 at the start of World War II. It was also used in 1970 as a result of two terrorists kidnappings in Montréal, Québec, called the October Crisis.

Women and Discrimination

Emily Murphy wrote many books and articles under the pen name Janey Canuck.

In the last century, women in many countries have had limited rights. In Canada, a woman lived under the authority of her father until she turned twenty-one. Once she married, all her property and wages belonged to her husband. As women did not have the right to vote, they were unable to change the laws that discriminated against them.

Through the twentieth century, women have gradually increased their rights. Industrialization resulted in better education for more women. During wartime, women did the work of men who were fighting overseas. In 1918, Canadian women achieved the right to vote in federal elections.

In 1929, an Alberta judge named Emily Murphy was challenged on her

FURTHER UNDERSTANDING
Maternity Leave

Employers must now give pregnant women a leave of absence called maternity leave, which can be taken before and/or after the baby is born. At one time, women could be fired from their jobs if they became pregnant. Many employers now have a standard leave of absence for men as well as women when their children are born.

authority to hear a case because she was a woman. In a famous court judgment by the Privy Council in Great Britain, at the time the highest court of appeal for Canadians, she successfully fought to make women "persons" under the law.

In the 1960s, women spoke out against unequal opportunities in Canadian society. As a result, the government changed some federal laws and included gender equality in the Canadian Human Rights Act in 1978.

HISTORY

The Persons Case

The Persons Case is one of the most famous cases in Canadian legal history. Five Alberta women—Henrietta Muir Edwards, Nellie McClung, Louise McKinney, Irene Parlby, and Emily Murphy—brought the case to the Supreme Court of Canada. These women, who became known as the Famous Five, asked the Supreme Court of Canada to declare that women were persons under the British North America Act (BNA) and, as a result, that they were eligible to be appointed to the senate.

The Supreme Court judges decided that the Act did not include women. It interpreted the BNA Act in light of the times in which it was written.

The Court said that women had been excluded in 1867, and they would be excluded in 1928. The justices pointed out that all nouns, pronouns, and adjectives in the BNA Act were masculine, and therefore, men were meant to govern Canada.

After speaking with several lawyers, and with

Nellie McClung gave fiery speeches in favour of giving women the right to vote.

the support of the government of Alberta and the prime minister, the five women appealed to the British Privy Council, which was Canada's highest court of appeal at the time.

On October 18, 1929, the five Lords of the Judicial Committee stated that the word "persons" in Section 24 includes both males and females. They stated that excluding women from public office was a "relic of days more barbarous than ours."

The Persons Case made it possible for women to become senators of Canada and members of other federal bodies. However, none of the original five women were ever appointed to the senate.

Today, Canadians celebrate "Person's Day," and since 1979, several women are awarded Person's Day medals each year.

Aboriginal Peoples and Discrimination

■ *The vote was extended to all Aboriginal Peoples in July 1960. The first Aboriginal Peoples to vote were members of the Rice Lake Band in Ontario, in October 1960.*

FURTHER UNDERSTANDING

Aboriginal Self-government

Many Aboriginal Peoples wish to see some form of self-government. The idea behind self-government is that Aboriginal Peoples would control the institutions that directly affect their lives. Government structures, health care, education, and the justice system would be controlled by Aboriginal Peoples. Many problems Aboriginal Peoples experience are related to the fact that many institutions are run according to the values of a different culture. Self-government would put Aboriginal Peoples in control of their own lives and allow them to rebuild their society according to the values of traditional Aboriginal life.

By the late twentieth century, about 4.3 percent of Canada's population, or 1,200,000 people, were Aboriginal Peoples, including Inuit and Métis. The exact status of Aboriginal Peoples in Canada remains uncertain. Historically, they were not treated as full Canadian citizens, either by British or Canadian governments. Until after World War II, for example, most Aboriginal Peoples were not allowed to vote.

The Aboriginal Peoples negotiated with the federal government when the 1982 Constitution was being drafted. It was not possible at that time to arrive at a definition of Aboriginal status. Instead, a clause in the Constitution ensures that Aboriginal status remains unaffected by the Constitution.

A fundamental issue is the belief of some Aboriginal Peoples that they have the right to self-determination. This means they believe they have the right to choose their own form of government and organize it according to their own political beliefs. Their government would negotiate with the Canadian government like any other foreign country.

Another issue is land ownership and use. For many centuries, Aboriginal Peoples lived in the area now called Canada. When settlers arrived, Aboriginal Peoples could not use the land as they had in the past. This had profound effects on their social and economic life. Aboriginal groups are dissatisfied with the way land use has been decided and the way in which resource rights and revenues have been divided.

Aboriginal groups are also concerned about their cultural survival. They want their status as a minority group preserved in law so they may conserve their cultural traditions, including their religions and languages.

Aboriginal Women and the Indian Act

During the 1970s and early 1980s, a group of Aboriginal women worked to overturn legislation that denied them many rights as Aboriginal Canadians. By using peaceful **lobbying**, they drew attention to their cause and brought about important changes to Canada's Indian Act.

Until 1985, Canada's Indian Act said that any Aboriginal woman who married a non-Aboriginal man would lose her Aboriginal status. The woman also lost all the Aboriginal rights set out in the Indian Act: her property on her reserve, her right to live on the reserve, voting rights on the reserve, band membership, and education benefits. Her children lost their status and rights as well.

Some women thought this was an unjust law because an Aboriginal man married to a non-Aboriginal woman did not lose his rights or status. In fact, his wife and children gained status as Aboriginals.

In 1970, an Ojibwa woman named Jeanette Lavell married a non-Aboriginal man and lost her status. She appealed to the Federal Court of Canada, but her case was rejected.

Another woman, Yvonne Bédard, was evicted from her reserve after marrying a non-Aboriginal man. Like Lavell, she felt this was unfair treatment.

In 1973, both Lavell and Bédard appealed to the Supreme Court, claiming that Canada's Bill of Rights assured everyone equality under the law. The Supreme Court ruled that the Indian Act was valid and did not discriminate against women. The decision angered many people.

In 1977, an Aboriginal woman from the Tobique reserve in New Brunswick filed a complaint against the Canadian government with the United Nations (UN). In 1981, the UN Human Rights Committee ruled that Canada's Indian Act violated the rights of Aboriginal women. The Canadian government said the Indian Act would be revised, but nothing happened.

A small group of women from the Tobique reserve continued to lobby the government. At first, they worked at the reserve level and visited reserves throughout New Brunswick. They formed a provincial group called the New Brunswick Native Women's Council. They worked with other Aboriginal and women's groups at the national level. One national women's group published a pamphlet about their concerns.

The Tobique women spoke to people throughout Canada. They met with premiers, members of Parliament, and cabinet ministers. They asked many citizens to join their lobbying efforts. Support for the women grew. Even women from the United States sent protest letters to Ottawa.

In 1984, the Liberal government introduced a bill that would give Aboriginal women and their children full Aboriginal status. This bill was stopped by Charlie Watt, an Aboriginal senator.

In 1985, the Conservative government introduced a similar bill. By this time, the Tobique women had won the support of several premiers and cabinet ministers. The new bill passed and became an amendment to the Indian Act in 1985.

The amendment gave full Aboriginal status to anyone who was born with it or had lost it for any reason. No band was allowed to deny women full status. Despite strong opposition, Aboriginal women achieved recognition of their right to lasting Aboriginal status by forming an effective group to lobby the government.

■ *As a result of Lavell and Bédard's actions, Aboriginal women were inspired to speak up for their rights.*

Mapping Canada's Immigrants

Seventy-five percent of immigrants to Canada settle in Montreal, Toronto, and Vancouver. Some people immigrate to Canada for economic reasons and to reunite with families. Other people immigrate for political reasons. A 2001 Statistics Canada study found that 91 percent of new immigrants planned to stay in Canada permanently and become Canadian citizens.

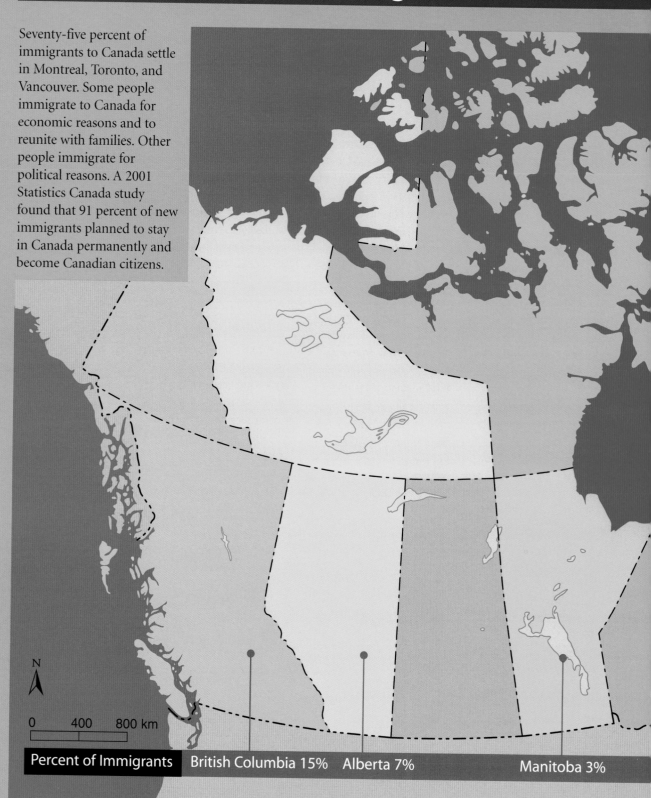

N

0   400   800 km

Percent of Immigrants   British Columbia 15%   Alberta 7%   Manitoba 3%

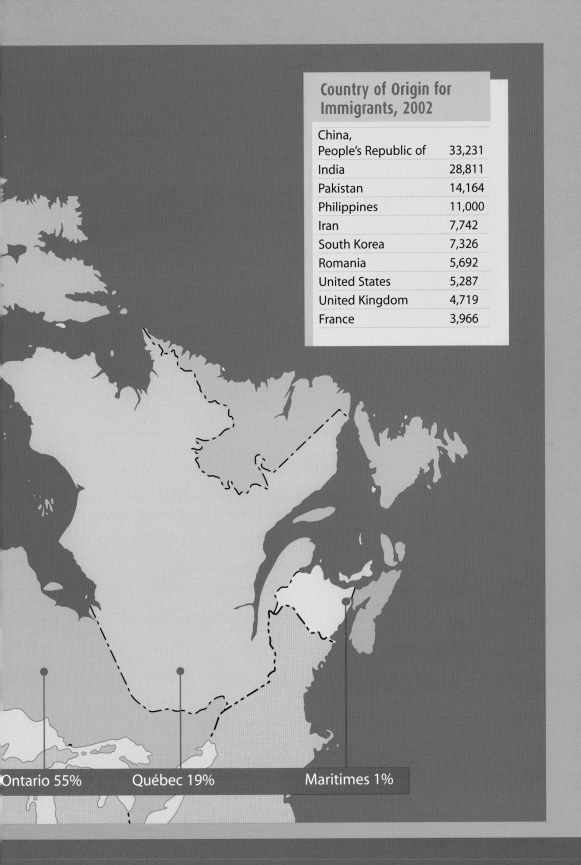

Country of Origin for Immigrants, 2002	
China, People's Republic of	33,231
India	28,811
Pakistan	14,164
Philippines	11,000
Iran	7,742
South Korea	7,326
Romania	5,692
United States	5,287
United Kingdom	4,719
France	3,966

Ontario 55%   Québec 19%   Maritimes 1%

Fostering Tolerance

Some Canadians make individual efforts to educate their fellow citizens and encourage tolerance and acceptance.

Cultural performances, such as traditional dances, help foster an understanding of other cultures.

The government has taken measures to prevent the reoccurrence of the types of discrimination that took place in the past. The Canadian Bill of Rights (1960) was the first of a number of important Canadian human rights laws that include provincial legislation like Alberta's Individual's Rights Protection Act (1972), the Canadian Human Rights Act (1977), and the Charter of Rights and Freedoms (1982).

Governments and institutions have implemented public policies such as affirmative action and employment equity to address problems of discrimination against disadvantaged groups and visible minorities, such as women, Aboriginal Peoples, and people with disabilities. In some regions, agencies such as police forces provide race-relations training programs for their staff and have created citizen

ACTIVE CITIZENSHIP

Celebrating Cultural Heritage

In Calgary, one group of Canadians uses Black History Month as an opportunity to discuss their cultural heritage and to explore stereotypes.

When Genevieve Balogun's son studied history in Grade 9, he decided to do a project on an Arctic explorer. There was nothing unusual in that, except the explorer he chose was Matthew Henson, an African American who ventured to the North Pole in 1909 with Robert Peary.

Balogun is president of the Calgary chapter of the Congress of Black Women, which organizes Black History Month in Calgary. She says the month is important "because it reminds us of our rich history that is so often lost in the shuffle." It is a chance, especially for the younger generation, to celebrate the accomplishments of Blacks. Everyone from Martin Luther King Jr., the American civil rights leader, to George Washington Carver, the inventor of peanut butter, is recognized.

The idea behind all the events is to celebrate the diversity of Blacks in Calgary. Balogun points out that Black Africans have a very different culture from Blacks who grew up in Caribbean countries and from those raised in the United States.

"We have in common our skin colour, but our background and experiences are very different," she says. "We are Canadians first and foremost, but we have brought our heritage with us and we can't leave it behind."

Balogun sees Black History Month as an opportunity for the Black community to talk about their experiences and explore stereotypes about themselves.

During his 1985 to 1987 Man In Motion World Tour, Rick Hansen wheeled over 40,000 kilometres through thirty-four countries on four continents. Hansen has raised more than $158 million for spinal cord injury research.

FURTHER UNDERSTANDING

Racism

Prejudice or discrimination against people of a particular race or ethnic background is called racism. Groups targeted by racism are often not allowed to participate fully in society because of the prejudice against them. Some forms of racism can be dealt with by laws that protect people from racist behaviour. It is illegal, for example, to refuse to rent an apartment to someone because of their skin colour. Most provinces have human rights commissions to deal with complaints of discrimination and racism. However, racism is an attitude, and it is hard to change attitudes with laws. Some forms of racism are so subtle that laws cannot deal with them. Sometimes people are guilty of racism without realizing it. The real key to ending racism and discrimination is to learn to treat all people with respect and dignity. Canadian schools, cities, community groups, clubs, and hospitals participate each year in the International Day for the Elimination of Racial Discrimination.

review boards to investigate complaints. Educators across the country have changed provincial curricula to reflect and promote acceptance of diversity.

Individual citizens also work to increase tolerance in their communities. Volunteers help organize multicultural festivals in towns and cities across the country. These festivals allow people from different cultures to learn about each other. Church groups and social agencies work to ensure equal opportunity for minority groups in simple ways, such as providing translation services.

Other Canadians make individual efforts to educate their fellow citizens and encourage tolerance and acceptance. For example, wheelchair athlete Rick Hansen wheeled around the world in his "Man in Motion World Tour" to raise awareness about the potential of people with disabilities.

Even though Canadians have made an effort to protect rights and freedoms with their laws, discrimination still negatively affects individuals belonging to minority groups and limits their full and equal participation in our society. However, if people know what their rights are and are willing to exercise them, society can reduce the harmful effects of discrimination.

Becoming a Canadian Citizen

■ *On special occasions, such as Canada Day, the governor general of Canada will often swear in new Canadian citizens.*

Citizenship gives Canadians full rights to participate in and contribute to Canadian life. If you were born in Canada and have spent all your life here, you may not have thought about what your Canadian citizenship means. Many people begin to think about their citizenship when they travel outside the country. If you live in Canada, but are not yet a Canadian citizen, you may be especially aware of what citizenship in this country means.

Canadian citizens enjoy full political participation through the rights to vote and run as candidates in federal or provincial elections. Citizens can travel abroad with a Canadian passport and have the right to return to Canada. They have the right to work and may hold some professional, business, or public service positions available only to Canadians. In return for these rights, citizens must be loyal to Canada.

If you were born in Canada, you are a natural citizen. Your birth certificate proves your citizenship. If you were born in another country and choose to become a citizen of Canada, you are a naturalized citizen. Both natural and naturalized citizens have the same rights, privileges, and responsibilities.

Naturalization is the way in which a person who comes to Canada to live permanently—called a landed immigrant—receives the rights, status, and privileges of Canadian citizenship. Landed immigrants may apply to become citizens by following the procedures set out by the Canadian government.

Landed immigrants must meet the requirements set out by the Citizenship Act:

- They must be 18 years or older to apply,
- lawfully admitted as a landed immigrant,
- be a resident in Canada for 3 years within the 4 years immediately before their application for citizenship,
- know either English or French,
- understand the rights and responsibilities of a Canadian,
- show an adequate knowledge of Canadian history, geography, and politics,
- not pose a threat to the security of Canada,
- not be on probation or parole, in prison, or convicted of an indictable offence within the past 3 years, and
- take the Oath of Citizenship.

A landed immigrant applies for citizenship at a citizenship court office. After completing the application form, the applicant arranges for an interview, or hearing, with a citizenship judge. The judge decides whether the applicant meets the requirements for citizenship. After a successful hearing, the court asks the applicant to attend a citizenship ceremony. This ceremony is a special event presided over by a judge.

The judge makes a speech about the benefits and responsibilities of Canadian citizenship, and the applicants swear the Oath of Canadian Citizenship. New Canadian citizens receive a certificate that proves their Canadian citizenship. Some people have plural citizenship, which means they are citizens of more than one country. In some cases, Canada allows people to keep their Canadian citizenship as well as their citizenship in another country. For example, if your French parents were working in Canada when you were born, you would have dual citizenship, both French and Canadian. Except in unusual circumstances, Canadians remain citizens for the rest of their lives.

In 1987, Prime Minister Brian Mulroney declared the week of April 17 National Citizenship Week to coincide with the proclamation of the Canadian Charter of Rights and Freedoms, which was signed into law on April 17, 1982. Citizenship is now celebrated during the third week of October. Canadian citizens can attend reaffirmation ceremonies held across Canada. At these ceremonies, Canadian citizens repeat the Oath of Citizenship to express their commitment to Canada.

FURTHER UNDERSTANDING

Oath of Canadian Citizenship

Canadian citizenship applicants repeat the Oath of Citizenship at special citizenship ceremonies:

I swear (or affirm) that I will be faithful and bear true allegiance to Her Majesty Queen Elizabeth the Second, Queen of Canada, Her Heirs and Successors, according to law and that I will faithfully observe the laws of Canada and fulfill my duties as a Canadian citizen.

During Citizenship and Heritage Week, some people receive a Citation for Citizenship award for helping new citizens integrate into their new communities.

Participatory Citizenship

Canadians participate in society in many different ways.

Participation lies at the heart of Canadian citizenship and democracy. Canadians have the right to vote, so they have the responsibility to be involved in choosing the people who make laws and who decide how things work in our society.

Canadians participate in society in many different ways. Some Canadians commit a great deal of time and energy organizing petitions or running for office in an election. Others attend meetings or write letters to the editors of newspapers and magazines to express their political views. Still others inform themselves about issues of concern or discuss politics with friends and neighbours. Most Canadian citizens participate by voting. Sixty-one percent of Canadians voted in the 2004 federal election.

Generally, there are two types of political participation in our country: influencing political decision making and sharing political power.

Citizens can influence political decision making by signing petitions, writing letters to editors, politicians, and public officials, participating in peaceful demonstrations or protests, lobbying bureaucrats and politicians on behalf of a group or issue, and voting. Some people do not believe these types of activities influence decision making. However, politicians and government officials listen to the views of their constituents. The more input politicians and government officials receive from people, the better chance the public's ideas will be adopted and reflected in laws and policies. Our political process depends on participation.

In the 2000 election, 80 percent of Canadians over the age of 58 voted. Only 22 percent of eligible 18-20 year olds cast a ballot.

Some people want to share decision-making power by becoming directly involved in the political process. You can do this by joining a political party, campaigning for a candidate in an election, running for election, or voting.

Not all people have the time or interest to join a political party or run for office. Voting, however, is an easy and significant way for all citizens to participate in politics. As a voter, you must make an effort to learn about issues and candidates. Some people do not vote because they feel their vote is not important in the larger scheme of society, but no one can predict the outcome of an election. Sometimes candidates win an election by only one or two votes.

Citizens have many opportunities to be involved. Generally, there are two main areas of participation: volunteering in your community and working to influence political decision making.

Community involvement typically consists of volunteering in groups or organizations that help improve life for you and your family in your neighbourhood or community. For example, you can serve on your local school council and community association to provide programs that improve the quality of life at your school and in your neighbourhood.

Political participation is also important. Government decisions affect everyone's lives. A democratic society provides its citizens with the opportunity to influence government decisions. Change happens through the participation of citizens in the political process. To make changes, you must find ways to be involved.

IN-DEPTH

How to Vote

1. Make sure your name appears on the voter list.
2. If you are not on the voter list, you can register during a 28-day period just before the election, at an advance polling station, or at a polling station on election day.
3. If you register on election day, you need identification, proof of residence, and a registered voter to vouch for you.
4. You will receive a voter information card showing the address of your polling station. If you do not receive a voter information card, you can call the returning office in your electoral district.
5. If you are unable to vote on election day, you may be able to vote in advance. This usually applies to people

■ *A returning officer is responsible for the successful running of an election in his or her area.*

who will be out of the country on election day.
6. On election day, you go to your polling station. There you will be given a ballot paper.
7. You vote by secret ballot in a private polling booth.
8. You make a clear mark in the circle by the name of the candidate you prefer.
9. A polling station official puts your folded ballot into a ballot box.
10. The ballots are counted after the polls close. The results are announced to the public.

Lobbying

Typically, lobby groups work to promote certain causes and have government policy reflect their own specific interests.

■ *Lobbyists usually have to register themselves so everyone knows who they are, what they represent, and what they do.*

FURTHER UNDERSTANDING

Factors Affecting the Success of Pressure Groups

- size of the group
- social status of the members
- cohesion of the group
- commitment of the members
- effectiveness of the group leadership
- support of key members of the community
- press coverage
- support of influential politicians
- community support for the group's values
- availability of funds

When groups of citizens try to influence government decisions and priorities, their activity is described as lobbying. Typically, lobby groups work to promote certain causes and to make government policy reflect their own specific interests. Lobby groups exist for almost every kind of special interest in our society. There are labour unions, environmental groups, business and professional associations, and agricultural and cultural groups.

Lobby groups have long been part of Canadian politics. Politics is partly a power struggle between **interest groups**. As a result, lobby groups play an important role in the decisions governments make by getting their message across to both the government and the public. If the government thinks the majority of Canadians feel a certain way about an issue, it will generally try to make a decision that pleases the majority.

Lobbying can take many forms. Lobby groups arrange informal meetings with government ministers and senior bureaucrats. They prepare formal presentations for government committees and, on occasion, review draft policies. Lobby groups organize demonstrations, workshops, meetings, and media campaigns to draw public attention to particular issues. They also sponsor research that benefits the public and provide information about government policies to the public through newsletters published for members.

Some groups hire professional lobbyists to promote their interests. Lobbyists use special skills and information to get their group's message to government officials. Many lobbyists are former government officials or politicians who understand how decisions are made. Recently, the federal government has begun to regulate paid lobbyists and restrict the way former bureaucrats and politicians participate in lobbying. Some people feel that professional lobbyists' influence can be so powerful that it actually impedes democracy rather than helping it.

Successful lobby groups are typically well funded and well connected to government decision makers. Some people argue that lobby groups should not be funded by the government under any circumstances. It seems strange to many that the government gives money to an organization that will try to influence its own policies.

Others argue that some interest groups represent people who cannot afford to fund their own lobby group. If government cannot help them, these people will lack an effective voice for their concerns.

Most lobby groups represent causes most politicians can support. Lobby groups are not always successful. Many conflicting interests exist in society, so government cannot satisfy everyone all the time. Government must try to consider the public's interest against those of special interest groups when it makes decisions.

IN-DEPTH

Pressure Group Tactics

Pressure groups use a number of tactics to reach their goals. Their lobbying is most often aimed at high-ranking civil servants, as well as elected officials. Lobbying includes making formal presentations, offering support in the next election, threatening to withdraw political support, organizing letter-writing campaigns, or holding public education events. Making a formal presentation to the government in the form of a brief is done on a regular basis by many organized groups in Canada.

While much lobbying with government occurs through meetings, telephone calls, letters, and formal presentations, there are other forms of pressure that can have the same effect.

Many pressure groups rely on the media to win public support for their views. Media advertising and press conferences are often used to inform the public and pressure the government. This is particularly true when government officials openly disagree with a pressure group's point of view. The two sides use the media to fight for public support.

Strikes are often used to protest government policies or legislation, and they are also used by people to win better wages or working conditions. Strikes often include demonstrations, picketing, and publishing brochures. These tactics are

■ *Withholding labour to obtain better working conditions is known as a strike.*

also used as protest measures when there is no strike. In some cases, a boycott will be organized to ask consumers not to buy certain products or not to buy products from certain companies.

Government Response to Participation

More Canadians are demanding a say in the decision-making process that affects areas such as the environment, health care, and education. Governments are responding to this demand by making public involvement part of the decision-making process. Governments use opinion polls and surveys, referendums or popular votes on specific issues, public meetings, workshops and hearings, presentations by groups with special interests, and task forces to obtain public input. Private companies and community groups also use some of these methods to involve people in making decisions.

Governments face the challenge of making public participation meaningful in their decision-making process. Increasingly, people want to know governments are considering their views carefully. There are many obstacles to shared, cooperative decision making. Not all citizens have the time, interest, or money to participate in the decision-making process. Shared decision making is a goal toward which governments and individuals must increasingly strive.

Occasionally, individuals receive concrete benefits for participating in society. The federal and provincial governments give tax deductions to

Members of Free the Children collected many signatures for their petition to stop child labour in developing countries.

people who donate money to political parties.

More often, the benefits of participation are less immediate. Communities and governments reward volunteers and service groups with awards of recognition.

Most people who participate get satisfaction from working with others to improve life in their communities. Whatever the benefits, participation is a central ingredient in our society and an important responsibility of all Canadians.

IN-DEPTH

Opinion Polls

Most citizens have political opinions, but they do not have the time, money, or connections to form a successful political party. Politicians, the media, and political parties often use opinion polls to find out how people feel about issues. In many cases, a poll is used as a decision-making tool.

Most major political parties hire polling companies to conduct polls on their behalf. These polls often consist of telephone interviews with a sample, or a group of people who represent a larger group. Poll results are used to assess voters' views about candidates, leaders, issues, and policies. Polls can be very useful during elections, when parties are trying to gauge public support and politicians are trying to decide what issues are important to people.

Governments often use polls to decide when to call an election because modern methods of sampling make most polls seem very reliable. It has been proven, however, that how voters answer a poll question might not reflect how they will vote. During the 1984 federal election campaign, for example, only one of eleven major polls reported in the newspapers accurately predicted the election results.

Polls can provide important and interesting

■ *New methods of surveying the public can be quite costly.*

information about what people think, and sometimes, they can show a trend developing in people's voting preferences or in the way an issue is perceived. However, polls can also be wrong, either due to the polling technique used or the changing nature of public opinion.

Media and Politics

Many Canadians do not get directly involved in the political system or by studying the issues in detail. Instead, they rely on the mass media—newspapers, magazines, radio, television, and the Internet—to help form their beliefs and views about politics.

Ideally, the media provides people with facts and opinions they need to make up their minds about issues that concern them. The media also helps individuals have a voice in the political process. For example, you can express your views by writing a letter to the editor. You can call a radio phone-in show. Reporters often interview ordinary citizens for their reactions to recent government decisions.

Governments sometimes use the media to receive information about public opinion of their decisions. More often, governments provide details about programs and policies to the public through the media. Television and radio broadcasts often include interviews with political leaders and clips from government press conferences. Occasionally, the government pays for newspaper space or broadcast time to deliver its message to citizens.

The media is closely woven into the daily fabric of our lives, and it can have a great deal of influence. Almost all Canadian homes have at least one radio and television set, and most towns and cities have a local newspaper. People rely on the media to make many decisions in their lives.

For this reason, some people worry about the amount of power the media has and the way it is used to influence people's ideas and actions. One area of concern is the media's role in elections. The media provides extensive coverage of federal and provincial elections,

Ninety-three percent of Canadian households own an FM radio, and 98 percent of households have a television.

ACTIVE CITIZENSHIP

Barbara Frum

People respond to personal challenges in different ways. For journalist Barbara Frum, an 18-year battle with leukemia strengthened her commitment to Canadians and spurred her to become one of the country's most skilful journalists.

When Barbara Frum entered broadcast journalism in 1967, she had no idea that most of her career would be spent battling leukemia.

In 1974, Frum was in her third year as host of CBC radio's *As It Happens* when she was diagnosed with leukemia. The diagnosis did not drive Frum away from her job.

Frum spent 11 years as the host of *As It Happens* and another 10 years as host of CBC television's *The Journal*, a nightly current affairs program. She devoted herself to explaining news to Canadians, and she often worked 13-hour days preparing and taping interviews.

During her years with *The Journal*, Frum interviewed thousands of

"After Frum, it was simply accepted without question that women could do serious interviews."

people, from national leaders to teenagers and athletes. She used tough, direct questions to cut straight to the heart of the issue. Many called her aggressive, but fair.

Frum died of leukemia on March 26, 1992, at the age of 54. When word of her death reached the media,

stories were filled with reflections about how her struggle to live underlined her direct, honest, no-nonsense approach to interviews. Indeed, she once told a reporter, "I think my situation makes me more empathetic and more attuned to people. You want to go deeper, and you realize that everyone's got something that torments them."

Following the news of Frum's death, the *Globe and Mail* television critic wrote that for 20 years Frum not only linked Canadians to national and global events, but she also explored important, timely issues that helped define what it means to be Canadian. Some journalists and colleagues hailed her as a role model for women. "She was a pioneer for women in broadcast journalism," said Mark Starowicz, executive producer for *The Journal*. "After Frum, it was simply accepted without question that women could do serious interviews."

including publicizing the results of public opinion polls. The use of polls by the media is a controversial issue. Some people suggest that polls do more to shape opinion than reflect opinion.

In addition, a British Columbia court ruling lifted the blackout of election results in areas where people were still voting for the 2004 federal election. Some people believe this could influence voters in close elections.

People are also concerned about the amount of propaganda in the media.

Propaganda is a mixture of fact, opinion, and assumptions meant to promote a particular plan and directly influence people's decisions. Some propaganda is easy to spot. Manufacturers use paid advertisements to convince you to buy their products. Groups, political parties, and governments also use the media to sell their ideas and programs. Sometimes, it is not easy to sort through what is propaganda, what is opinion, and what is factual information.

Universal Declaration of Human Rights

The Declaration was a statement to the world outlining how citizens, governments, and organizations should treat each other.

In 1948, shortly after World War II ended, the United Nations created and adopted its Universal Declaration of Human Rights. The Declaration was a statement to the world outlining how citizens, governments, and organizations should treat each other. Many people called the declaration "The Magna Carta of Mankind," and many viewed it as a renewed commitment to peace and justice around the world.

The declaration lists thirty fundamental rights that should be guaranteed to everyone, regardless of race, nationality, religion, age, or gender. These rights include social, political, economic, civil, and cultural rights, as well as freedoms. Some of the rights listed are well-known "traditional" or "old" rights. For example, the declaration states that no one should be tortured or punished in a cruel, inhuman, or degrading way. It also states that everyone is equal in the eyes of the law and that everyone must be guaranteed protection by the law.

Other rights in the declaration are "contemporary" or "new" rights. These rights include the right to rest and leisure, the right to education, and the right to enjoy the arts and participate in cultural events. By mixing old rights with new rights, the declaration tries to state what people need in order to live with freedom and dignity in any society.

Over the years, many countries have used the declaration to create their own charters of rights and freedoms. Many countries have also used the declaration to develop their own constitutions and laws or to make court decisions. Today, many countries view the declaration as a challenge they must meet.

The UN flag features a world map surrounded by an olive branch. The olive branch symbolizes peace. On the UN flag, the olive branch symbolizes world peace.

DOCUMENT

The Universal Declaration of Human Rights

All human beings are born free and equal in dignity and rights.

Everyone is entitled to all the rights and freedoms set forth in this Declaration, without distinction of any kind, such as race, colour, gender, language, or religion.

Everyone has the right to life, liberty, and security of person.

No one shall be held in slavery; slavery and the slave trade shall be prohibited in all their forms.

No one shall be subjected to torture or to cruel, inhuman, or degrading treatment or punishment.

All are equal before the law and are entitled without any discrimination to equal protection of the law.

Everyone charged with a penal offence has the right to be presumed innocent until proved guilty.

Everyone has the right to freedom of movement and residence within the borders of each State.

Everyone has the right to leave any country and return.

Men and women of full age, without any limitation due to race, nationality, or religion, have the right to marry and found a family.

Everyone has the right to own property.

Everyone has the right to freedom of thought, conscience, and religion.

Everyone has the right to freedom of opinion and expression.

Everyone has the right to freedom of peaceful assembly and association.

Everyone has the right to equal pay for equal work.

Everyone has the right to form and to join trade unions.

Everyone has the right to rest and leisure.

Everyone has the right to education.

Everyone has the right to participate freely in the cultural life of the community and to enjoy the arts.

Time Line

1215 King John of England signs the Magna Carta, which is Latin for the "Great Charter."

1628 King Charles I of England signs the Petition of Rights. This document challenged the idea of the divine right of kings.

1689 The English Bill of Rights is signed. This document further limits the power of the monarchy and protects the rights of individuals.

1789 The Declaration of the Rights of Man is passed by the National Assembly of France.

1791 The United States Bill of Rights is ratified by three-quarters of the state legislatures.

1867 The British Parliament passes the British North America Act. This act establishes the Canadian Confederation.

1918 Canadian women are given the right to vote in federal elections.

1929 Canadian women are declared "persons" by the Judicial Committee of the Privy Council in England.

1948 The United Nations creates its Universal Declaration of Human Rights.

1949 Canadians of Asian and Indian heritage are given the right to vote.

1960 The Canadian Bill of Rights is passed.

1960 Aboriginal Peoples in Canada are given the right to vote.

Canadian suffragettes

Pierre Trudeau with Richard Nixon

1992 Canadian referendum rejects Charlottetown Accord.

1995 Second referendum in Québec rejects independence by a 1 percent margin.

2001 Helmut Oberlander's Canadian citizenship is revoked by cabinet. He lied about serving as a translator for a Nazi death squad during World War II.

1967 The Order of Canada is created to honour Canadians who have enriched the lives of others.

1971 Prime Minister Pierre Trudeau makes multiculturalism Canada's official policy.

1977 Canadian Human Rights Act becomes law.

1982 The Canadian Charter of Rights and Freedoms is passed.

1987 Prime Minister Brian Mulroney declares the week of April 17 National Citizenship Week.

2004 The blackout on election results in areas where the polls are still open is lifted for federal election.

RCMP officer

Quiz (answers on page 47)

Multiple Choice

Choose the best answer in the multiple choice questions that follow.

1 Which political theory claims all human beings have certain rights?

a) communism
b) conservatism
c) natural human rights
d) liberalism

2 In which century was the Magna Carta signed?

a) seventeenth century
b) thirteenth century
c) twentieth century
d) eighteenth century

3 In what year did multiculturalism become Canada's official policy?

a) 1931
b) 1960
c) 1982
d) 1971

4 What award honours Canadians who have enriched the lives of others?

a) Governor General's Award
b) Stanley Cup
c) Order of Canada
d) Order of Merit

5 In what year did the Canadian Charter of Rights and Freedoms become law?

a) 1929
b) 1791
c) 1960
d) 1982

6 Alberta passed what human rights law in 1972?

a) Alberta Bill of Rights
b) Human Rights Act
c) Universal Declaration of Human Rights
d) Individual's Rights Protection Act

Mix and Match

Match the description in column A with the correct terms in column B. There are more terms than descriptions.

A	B
1. Made multiculturalism Canada's official policy	a) Japan
2. Declared Canadian women "persons"	b) King Charles I
3. Election results blackout lifted by this province's court.	c) Brian Mulroney
	d) Chinese
4. Prohibited from buying Alberta farm land in 1944	e) Pierre Trudeau
	f) Aboriginal Peoples
5. Attacked Pearl Harbor in 1941	g) British Columbia
6. Declared the week of April 17, 1987, National Citizenship Week	h) Hutterites
	i) Judicial Committee of the Privy Council of England

Time Line

Find the appropriate spot on the time line for each event listed below.

A United Nations creates Universal Declaration of Human Rights.

B Canadian Human Rights Act becomes law.

C Canadians of Asian and Indian heritage are given the right to vote.

D The English Bill of Rights is signed by King Charles I.

E United States Bill of Rights ratified.

F Aboriginal Peoples of Canada are given the right to vote.

1215 Magna Carta is signed by King John of England.
1689 1
1789 Declaration of the Rights of Man is passed by the National Assembly of France.
1791 2
1867 British North America Act is passed by British Parliament.
1918 Canadian women are given the right to vote in federal elections.

1929 Canadian women are declared "persons."
1948 3
1949 4
1960 Canadian Bill of Rights is passed.
1960 5
1967 The Order of Canada is created.
1971 Multiculturalism becomes Canada's official policy.
1977 6

1982 Canadian Charter of Rights and Freedoms becomes law.
1987 Week of April 17 is declared National Citizenship Week.
1992 Canadian referendum rejects Charlottetown Accord.
1995 Second referendum in Québec rejects independence by a 1 percent margin.

Further Research

Suggested Reading

Nicol, Eric. *Canadian Politics Unplugged.* Toronto: Dundurn Press, 2003.

Quinlan, Don, Mary Jane Pickup, and Terry Lahey. *Government: Participating in Canada.* Toronto: Oxford University Press, 1999.

Tammemagi, Hans. *Exploring the Hill: An Intimate Look at Canada's Parliament.* Toronto: Fitzhenry & Whiteside, 2002.

Tindal, C. Richard. *A Citizen's Guide to Government.* Toronto: McGraw-Hill Ryerson, 2000.

Internet Resources

Canada: A People's History Online
history.cbc.ca
The online companion to CBC's award-winning television series on the history of Canada, as told through the eyes of its people. This multimedia Web site features behind-the-scenes information, games, puzzles, and discussion boards. The site is also available in French.

The Canadian Encyclopedia Online
www.thecanadianencyclopedia.com
A reference for all things Canadian. In-depth history articles are accompanied by photographs, paintings, and maps. All articles can be read in both French and English.

Some Web sites stay current longer than others. To find other Web sites that deal with Canada's system of government, enter terms such as "House of Commons," "Senate," and "Supreme Court" into a search engine.

Glossary

bill: a proposed law brought before a provincial legislature or Parliament for reading, debate, study, and possible approval

citizenship: a process in which citizens participate in Canadian life at the individual, community, and societal level

democracy: a political system, sometimes called rule by the people, in which the people elect their government

discrimination: the act of treating someone differently, usually unfairly, because that person is seen as different from others

heritage: practices that are handed down from the past by tradition

human rights: rights that are considered basic to human dignity and life in society

interest groups: a group of people sharing one or more common concern and trying to further their interests by influencing governments at different levels

lobbying: the act of voicing opinions to lawmakers in government in order to influence their decisions

naturalization: the legal process through which a citizen of one country becomes a citizen of another

Parliament: the central government, composed of the House of Commons, the Senate, and the monarchy

participation: to take part or to share

political party: a group of people who share similar ideas about how government should operate

power: the ability to act, control, or influence

prejudice: an opinion formed by ignoring facts and information, and by refusing to take the time or care to judge fairly

responsibilities: obligations or duties for which a citizen is held accountable, such as serving on a jury, paying taxes, or obeying the laws

rights: privileges protected by law and agreed to belong to all citizens based on common beliefs about justice

Answers

Multiple Choice	Mix and Match	Time Line
1. c)	1. e)	1. d)
2. b)	2. i)	2. e)
3. d)	3. g)	3. a)
4. c)	4. h)	4. c)
5. d)	5. a)	5. f)
6. d)	6. c)	6. b)

Index

Aboriginal Peoples 7, 9, 11, 24, 25, 28, 42
Atwood, Margaret 13

Black History Month 28
Blainey, Justine 13

Canadian Pacific Railway 19
Charter of Rights and Freedoms 4, 5, 7, 10, 11, 12, 13, 14, 28, 31, 43
Chinese 9, 18, 19
Citizenship Act 5, 31
citizenship judge 4, 5, 31
constitution 7, 9, 10, 24, 40

English Bill of Rights 6, 7, 42

freedom of conscience and religion 7, 11, 17, 41
freedom of speech 10
Frum, Barbara 39

Hansen, Rick 29
human rights commissions 13, 14, 15, 16, 17, 29
Hutterites 17

Individual's Rights Protection Act (IRPA) 14, 15, 16, 17, 28

Japanese 20, 21

landed immigrant 30, 31
lobbying 25, 32, 34, 35

Magna Carta 6, 40, 42
media 11, 34, 35, 37, 38, 39
multiculturalism 8, 9, 43

National Citizenship Week 31, 43
natural human rights 6, 7
naturalization 30

opinion polls 36, 37, 39
Order of Canada 8, 43

Petition of Rights 6, 42
prejudice 5, 17, 18, 29
propaganda 38, 39

racism 29
responsibilities 4, 5, 8, 9, 30, 31
rights 4, 5, 6, 7, 8, 9, 10, 11, 12, 13, 14, 15, 16, 17, 18, 20, 22, 25, 29, 30, 31, 40, 41, 42

special interest groups 35

Ukrainians 20

voting 7, 9, 25, 32, 33, 37, 42

War Measures Act 20, 21
Women's Legal Education and Action Fund (LEAF) 13